Lost in Space

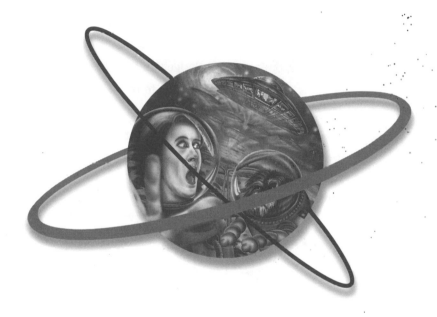

Thrillogy

Edited by Paul Collins and Meredith Costain

sundance

Read all of the
 Titles

Fantasy/Horror	Science Fiction
Dragon Tales	Alien Invasions
Ghosts and Ghoulies	Gadgets and Gizmos
Heroic Feats	It Came from the Lab . . .
Last Gasps	Lost in Space
Tales from Beyond	Techno Terror
Terrors of Nature	Time Zones

Published by Sundance Publishing
P.O. Box 1326, 234 Taylor Street, Littleton, MA 01460

First published 1999 as Spinouts by
Addison Wesley Longman Australia Pty Limited
95 Coventry Street, South Melbourne 3205 Australia
Exclusive United States Distribution: Sundance Publishing

ISBN 0-7608-4825-4

Printed in Canada

Contents

The Space Shed

The author
Dirk Strasser
talks about the story

"I remember playing 'space explorers' in our backyard when we were kids. We used to fly through meteor showers and land on alien planets. Of course, we were only *pretending* to be space explorers, weren't we? Then again, who knows."

The Space Shed

Adam raised his weapon and took aim at the
Vulags. I was still fooling around with mine when
Adam pressed the freeze button on his blaster.
He fired. The icy blast reached the scampering
creatures, and they froze instantly. Their bright
yellow bodies were now dulled by a covering of ice.

"We have to go," said Adam. "They won't stay frozen for long in this atmosphere. It's too hot."

"They don't really look so scary now, do they?" I said. "These Vulags might have sharp teeth, but they . . ."

"What are you doing?"

I walked up to the three Vulags, who were standing there like statues. "I just want to take a closer look."

"Derek, I've told you the rules of the Planet Exploration Service."

"I know. We found out what we need to know about the planet, and now we have got to get back to the ship." Adam could be such a pain, sometimes.

"Well, let's go then."

"But—hey!"

I jumped back. One of the Vulags had growled.

"It's too humid here," Adam said. "They're already waking up."

We took off through the jungle. I followed Adam's lead, but I was finding it hard to breathe because of the heat. Now and then, I heard scampering noises in the damp undergrowth, but I tried to ignore them. Vines hung from the trees like huge strands of green spaghetti, and I had to keep pushing them out of the way.

Adam stopped suddenly. He looked at the band around his wrist and frowned.

"What's wrong?" I asked. "I thought you said we had to get off this planet."

"There's moisture inside my locator."

"What does that mean?"

"I'm not sure in which direction the *Space Eagle* is."

"That's easy," I said. "It's . . . uh . . ." I turned all the way around, trying to figure out where we should be going.

Adam removed his wristband. "I think I can fix it."

There was a crashing noise in the treetops above us. I raised my blaster and looked up to see two red and gold birds fly off.

Adam grabbed me by the arm. "Never shoot at birds. You'll kill them. They fall to the ground when they're frozen."

"Sorry—I know the rules. They just made me jump, that's all."

The bushes to our left shook, and before we knew it, several Vulags were charging toward us. We fired our weapons and the creatures froze. I could hear more sounds from the bushes to my left. Adam signaled me to follow, and we took off.

Giant fern fronds and vines slapped my face as we jumped over roots and small bushes. It started drizzling and steam rose from the ground.

"Are we almost there?" I asked in between gasps.

"I don't really know—I'm only guessing."

The raindrops became heavier, and it was difficult to see for more than a few yards.

"It's like being in a giant shower," I said.

Adam didn't answer.

"Except," I added, "I've never been chased by a herd of Vulags in my shower." I could still hear some growls, but most of the jungle noises were being drowned out by the sound of the rain.

I screamed. Something had wrapped itself around my arm and was lifting me off the ground. I heard the hiss of Adam's blaster. As the vine around me froze, I realized I was now dangling in midair with the jungle floor fifteen feet below.

"Help me!" I cried as I looked down, but Adam was busy firing at a dozen Vulags coming at him through the rain.

By the time Adam had frozen them all, my shoulder was beginning to hurt.

"Hey, don't forget about me," I said.

"We've got a problem," said Adam, rubbing his chin the way he always did when he was thinking.

"What is it?"

"I don't know how I can get you down."

I reached up with my free hand and tried to snap the frozen vine.

"Don't do that."

"Why not?"

"You'll hurt it, maybe even kill it."

"What do you mean?"

"Planet Exploration rules. No killing. No injuring."

"I know that, but that's for animals, not plants."

"Yes, but I don't think the thing that's got you is a vine. It looks more like a snake."

"Oh great! So I just hang here until it unfreezes, and then I let it drag me up to its nest or something."

Adam rubbed his chin again. "Wait—I have an idea."

He adjusted the temperature button on his blaster to *melt*. "Now, I'm going to unfreeze it."

"Good idea, Adam, that way the snake can eat me a lot faster."

"There'll be a split second just after it unfreezes, when it won't know what's going on. Just unwrap the snake quickly, and you'll fall clear."

I wasn't sure if it was going to work, but I realized that I didn't have much choice. As Adam fired his blaster, I could feel the snake loosen around my arm. I grabbed the snake with my free hand and unwrapped it. The next thing I knew, I was sitting on the ground.

Adam reached down to help me up. "Let's find the *Space Eagle* before the snake tries to grab you again."

I rubbed my shoulder and looked up at the huge snake, which was now wriggling from side to side. We headed off, walking at first, but then running when we heard growls coming from the melting Vulags.

"I'm not sure I like this planet," I said.

After a few minutes of running, we stumbled into the clearing where we had landed the *Space Eagle*.

The rain had turned to drizzle again, and as we entered the ship, we could hear scurrying noises from the bushes around us.

I looked through the hatch just as it was sliding shut. Hundreds of Vulags were coming out from the undergrowth and moving toward the ship. I could hear scratching noises on the hull, as we

strapped ourselves into the flight control module and began the liftoff checks.

Moments later the *Space Eagle* took off, and Adam and I were on our way back to Earth.

I stepped out of the shed and blinked at the bright sunlight. Little pieces of cloud were floating across a clear blue sky.

"Another successful mission?" I asked as Adam came out behind me.

Adam nodded. He never seemed to speak much

once we were back on Earth. He also seemed to move more slowly, like he had to think carefully about everything he did.

"I don't think I ever want to see a Vulag again," I said.

Adam closed the shed door and very carefully pushed the small bolt into place.

"Have you picked the next planet?" I asked.

Adam looked at his feet.

"What's wrong?"

"Nothing, Derek."

Adam was being stranger than usual. I walked over to the fence separating our two yards. "I'll stop by after school as soon as I can. See ya." I pushed aside the broken slat in the fence and squeezed my way through to my own backyard.

It was a few days before I had the chance to see Adam again. Friday night came, and I climbed out of my bedroom window and headed next door. I squeezed through the back fence, and then gulped when I saw Adam's father watching me. I hadn't spoken to him much because he was away a lot—like Dad used to be before he and Mom split up.

"Where's Adam?" I asked, trying to sound cheerful.

"He's not well." His voice always sounded a little funny, like he had an accent.

"Can I see him?"

"He's inside," he said. "In his bedroom."

I walked past him and went inside. It always felt strange being in Adam's house, as if the furniture wasn't quite in the right place.

I went straight into Adam's room. He looked pale, and his eyes were sort of watery.

"When's our next mission?" I asked.

I heard Adam's father behind me. "There isn't going to be a next mission for you two," he said.

"Why?" I asked him.

"We have to move again. Please don't talk to Adam too long. He's very tired."

Adam's father left the room.

"We're leaving tomorrow," Adam said. "It's the gravity here. My body can't handle it anymore."

I looked at him anxiously. "But you could go to a doctor. They can fix anything."

Adam rubbed his chin slowly. "No," he said, "they can't fix gravity. Anyway, even if I were staying, we wouldn't be able to explore any more planets. Dad found out I was using the *Space Eagle* to take you on missions."

"Where are you going?"

"Wherever Dad gets sent."

We spoke a little more, but Adam's father soon came back, and I had to go.

I walked home, climbed through my bedroom window, and got into bed, exhausted.

The next morning I dressed quickly, then raced outside and squeezed through the fence into Adam's backyard.

Thank goodness the shed was still there. I opened the door, and the hinges creaked. The light was dim inside, but I could see stacks of cans, crates, and boxes. Dusty cobwebs hung in every corner. I looked down at where the flight control module had been, but all I could see were two broken crates. There was a stick on the ground next to one of them, and I picked it up. The words *freeze* and *melt* were written on it in blue letters.

I stepped outside into the sunshine for a moment, and then went back in again. But it was all still the same. I was going to call Adam's name, but I knew it was silly. He was gone.

Another family moved into Adam's house soon afterward. I don't squeeze through the hole in the fence anymore, mainly because I'm too big to fit. I feel kind of sad sometimes when I see the old shed. Once in a while I open the door and walk in. But it's never more than just an old shed.

Station
Starside One

The author
Sally Odgers
talks about the story

"Why do we do that? Why do we believe this? Gee, wow, it's tradition! Traditions fascinate me, so I wrote a story about one that was misunderstood and just worn out."

Station Starside One

Station Starside One sailed silently through its orbit. It was Earth's first space station. Its original voyagers long gone, it was now home to thousands of people. And every one of them had been born on the great ship that circled Earth.

At first, the Stationers maintained radio contact with Earth by means of a vid-link. But as the years passed, they became a city unto themselves and eventually saw no need to maintain communication with Earth. The vid-link screen was abandoned in the unused loading bay, its grav-shaft entrance boarded up.

Much later, Starsides Two and Three were launched. Space-skippers were invented and used for commuting back and forth to Earth. Earth Central considered offering skippers to the people of SS1, but what was the point? They never made contact now. They never responded to messages sent on the vid-link screen. Obviously, they wanted privacy.

Three centuries later, Hurryup fell through the rotted boards of SS1's abandoned grav-shaft. "Fall down, me!" he clanked. "Pria help Hurryup!"

"What is this place?" wondered Pria. It was a long way down, but Hurryup was her best friend, a present from Grandfather. She tested the grav-shaft by dropping a rusty bolt down it, then jumped in and drifted to the round, gray room below.

"Hurt, me." Hurryup creaked his metal limbs.

"No way," said Pria, hugging him. "Robo-pets are indestructible." The room was empty, with a round groove in the floor. Next to it was a panel in a swiveling frame. It was dull silver, covered with dust, and had sliding switches and dials on the top. The switches were stiff, but Pria turned one on, making the panel swirl and ripple. She tried a dial. It hardly moved, but the frame lit up and red letters began to blink on its rim.

"MAL-FUNCT-ION-MAL-FUNCT-ION-MAL-FUNCT-ION."

Hurryup whirred and clanked excitedly. "Pria, signal make!"

The letters were changing to amber as Pria backed away. "VID-TECH-DI-SPATCH-ING-VID-TECH-DI-SPATCH-ING." Then they were green. "VID-TECH-AR-RIV-ING-VID-TECH-AR-RIV-ING." The grooved section of floor fell away and a weird, round vehicle rose through the gap. Pria cowered against the wall as a figure disembarked, removed its helmet, and turned and smiled at her. It was a stranger, a boy about her own age.

"I'm Jik," he said. "I'm your vid-link screen service technician."

"You—you *what*?" she stammered.

"I'm a service technician, and you know what?

I qualified yesterday!" He grinned. "Never expected a call on my first day! What is this place?"

"SS1, of course."

"Space Station Starside One!" Jik whistled. "I didn't know this place had a vid-link screen!"

"A *what*?"

"Vid-link screen." Jik indicated the flashing panel. "When I picked up that malfunction beacon, I flipped the space-skipper to auto-track and hopped in. What's your name, and what's that you're holding?"

"I'm Pria, and this is Hurryup."

"No hurry me," clanked Hurryup.

Jik laughed, bending to examine the flashing screen. "Ugh—what a filthy antique! Gunk in the works, that's the trouble." Humming, he cleaned the panel, then adjusted the switches and dials. "That's better, but the focus is blurred. Which part of Earth shall we see, Pria?"

"Earth?" she said uncertainly. She had heard of Earth, of course, but she never expected to see it. "I don't know."

"I'll show you my home," decided Jik. He turned the dial. The screen brightened and a city swam into view, closer and closer, until Pria saw people in the streets.

"That looks like our city," she said. "But who are the people?"

"Wait." Jik twiddled the dial. The city shifted sideways. Now the view showed one house and a patch of green.

Pria cuddled Hurryup closely. "What are those big vegetables?"

"You mean trees?" said Jik.

"And that big stuff like water?"

"That's our pond." Jik stared at her. "Pria, haven't you used this screen before?"

"No one comes to the forgotten sector. Only us, because Hurryup fell down the grav-shaft."

Jik frowned as he adjusted the focus so Pria could see the pond.

"Oh!" said Pria longingly. "I've never seen anything like it!"

"Don't you get Earth-leave?" asked Jik. "Vacations on Earth?"

"How could we?"

"People from SS6 and SS7 do."

Pria couldn't imagine that. "They must be much closer to Earth," she said.

Weird! Jik knew SS1 was the closest of the far-range stations. But that vid-link screen *had* been badly corroded, and there'd never been a service call from SS1 before.

Security protocols meant no one from Earth could approach a station unless summoned by the Stationers' beacon. Had he made some terrible mistake?

"You called this place the forgotten sector. Does that mean forbidden?"

"I don't think so." Pria shook back her hair. "Let's ask Grandfather. He'll know."

"No. No, I don't think so." There were severe penalties for invading space stations without an invitation. "The screen's fine now," Jik said heartily. He adjusted the focus to the swirling "standby" pattern again. "I have to go. Good-bye." He clamped on his helmet.

"Wait," said Pria. "What about asking Grandfather?"

"Better not," said Jik. "Sorry, I shouldn't have come." Hurriedly, he sealed himself into the space-skipper and left the docking bay.

That beacon must have triggered accidentally. It wasn't his fault, but he hoped his supervisor would understand.

Pria knelt by the blank vid-link screen. Earth! Wouldn't it take a lifetime to reach it? No, because Jik lived there. She frowned as she clambered up the grav-shaft with Hurryup and ran to Grandfather's unit.

"Grandfather, what do you know about Earth?"

Grandfather looked surprised. "Not much, Pria. Why?"

"I met an Earthlie today." Pria explained about Jik and the vid-link screen.

Grandfather's eyebrows shot up to his ginger hair. "In the forgotten sector, you say? Amazing! I'll see what I can find out."

Soon, Grandfather found some answers. "According to the old records," said Grandfather, "SS1 is the earliest space station in the Starside System."

"Of course," scoffed Pria. "That's why it's Station Starside *One*."

"It took the Earthlies a hundred years to bring SS1 into this orbit," said Grandfather. "The first Stationers traveled all their lives to get here. They knew there was no return to Earth."

"There is now," said Pria. "If Jik could visit us, we could visit Earth!"

"Obviously." Grandfather sighed. "I suppose the idea of permanent exile was so strong that the first Stationers taught it to their descendants, and we've believed in it ever since! But Pria, you must face facts. The Earthlies don't want us to visit. If they did, they'd have invited us long ago."

"That's dumb!" said Pria.

Grandfather shrugged. "Traditions live longer than people, Pria."

"So? Just because a tradition is old doesn't mean it's good," she objected. "I'm going to visit Earth! Just you wait and see."

"How?" asked Grandfather.

"I'll find a way."

Back on Earth, Jik confessed his mistake to his supervisor. "Pria triggered the beacon accidentally, I guess. She didn't understand."

"No harm done," said Marko kindly. "You attended a malfunction call. That's what vid-techs do."

29

"Marko, why *don't* SS1 Stationers visit Earth?"

Marko shrugged. "I guess they like to keep to themselves, Jik."

"Pria has never seen a tree or a pond!"

"Presumably she doesn't want to. The SS1 Stationers have ignored us for centuries. They don't care about us."

"I could have invited Pria for a visit," muttered Jik. "You know, I think I will."

"You know the penalties for interfering, Jik!"

"I've been there once."

"Genuine mistakes can be overlooked, but *your* job is to service vid-link screens, not to upset people."

Pria was still determined to visit Earth, but *how?* She hoped Jik might come back and help her, but he didn't.

Grandfather couldn't help, so she and Hurryup spent hours in the old docking bay, trying to make the vid-link screen work. Sometimes Pria thought she saw fleeting glimpses of Earth, but she could never bring them into focus.

"This is so annoying, Hurryup! There must be *some* way to make it work!" she complained.

"MAL-FUNCT-ION-MAL-FUNCT-ION-MAL-FUNCT-ION," hummed Hurryup.

"Not any more. It's fixed. I just can't seem to make it work!"

"Pria signal make!" said Hurryup brightly.

"Another malfunction signal? I suppose I *could*." Pria grinned. "Clever, clever Hurryup! I've been trying to make it work right, but it really should work wrong!"

Pria tried all the switches and dials. They all moved easily, and nothing happened.

"Works gunk in," said Hurryup.

"No, Hurryup, Jik cleaned it . . ." Pria's voice trailed off as she realized what was wrong. She couldn't set off a malfunction beacon because the vid-link screen *wasn't* malfunctioning. The only reason it wouldn't work was because she didn't understand the controls. There was nothing *wrong* with it.

"Gunk in the works!" she shouted. "That's what we need!"

Pria swept up a pile of dust and rust and grit. She dampened it with oil from Hurryup's reserves, then rubbed it into the vid-link screen. Then she let it sit.

Two days later, she brought Grandfather to see the screen. And this time, when she tried the dials, something happened!

"MAL-FUNCT-ION-MAL-FUNCT-ION-MAL-FUNCT-ION," flashed the red letters.

Hurryup whirred and clanked excitedly as the words blinked amber, and finally, green. "Pria, signal make!"

"VID-TECH-DI-SPATCH-ING-VID-TECH-DI-SPATCH-ING. VID-TECH-AR-RIV-ING-VID-TECH-AR-RIV-ING."

Pria danced with glee as the floor dropped and the space-skipper rose into view.

The vid-tech got out and unclamped his helmet. "I know you're not interested in Earth," he began warily.

"That's silly!" said Pria. "Who told you that?"

"Marko says it's an old tradition," said Jik.

"A *bad,* old tradition." Pria grinned at him. "This is Grandfather, Jik, and of course you already know Hurryup. And guess what! The four of us are about to start a *new* tradition!"

Adrift

The author
Simon Brown
talks about the story

"I wrote this story because I have always been fascinated — well, terrified — by the thought of becoming lost in a great void: that of space, or under the ocean. And yes, I firmly believe that the first people to be born in space will not consider Earth to be their real home."

Simon Brown

Adrift

Uma flipped the gold filter down over her visor as she used her hands to pull herself across the day line. Her fingers found holds in the compacted lunar rock that made up the outer surface of Space Station *Plato's* hull. Bright sunlight bathed her. She looked up briefly and took in the view. The station was located at Lagrangian 1, between the earth and the moon.

From her position she could see the earth, distant and blue. The algae lining the surface of her biosuit slowly expanded their chlorophyll receptors to use the sunlight. Uma felt her skin start to heat up. But before she could become too warm, the suit got rid of the extra heat through the set of silicon spikes on her back. She reported in to the maintenance supervisor.

"Hey, Dad! I'm dayside."

"Don't forget communication protocol," came her father's voice, gently chiding.

"Sorry." She took a deep breath. "Maintenance, Uma Roe here. Have reached dayside."

"That was quick. Did you hitch a ride with one of the cargo scooters?"

"I've been practicing my hand-walking. It's faster than using boot spikes when you get the hang of it."

"You were born for space, Uma."

"That's what I'm always telling you," Uma said seriously.

Her father sighed. "Uma, you've got to go home for school."

"*Plato* is home, Dad. I was born here, remember?"

"I'm just worried about your future, darling."

"*Plato* is the future. I don't want to go to Earth. We have perfectly good schools here."

Her father changed the subject. "Do you have your scanner?"

Uma pulled the scanner from her utility belt and held it up to her visor. The tiny camera inside the faceplate transmitted its picture back to her father.

"I want you to go over the hull in that area. Seven hours ago, our instruments recorded an impact there with a larger-than-average micrometeoroid. Find the hole and report back."

"I'm on it!" Uma signed off.

She slowly moved down over the curve of the hull, and in a short time had covered most of the sector. She was about to give up the search when she saw a thin stream of vapor coming from the hull about ten yards from her position.

"Maintenance, Uma Roe here. I found your hole."

"Hi, Uma. Maintenance here. How big is it?"

"I'm not there yet, Dad, but it's leaking. Something more than the hull's been penetrated."

"Uh-oh. Can you get to it?"

Uma carefully hand-walked her way toward the hole. Even though she had a small jet pack on her belt to help push her back to safety if she drifted away from the station, she was always cautious. There was no point in asking for trouble. In the old days, the first settlers used safety lines for trips outside the station, but no colonist born on *Plato* would ever dream of using a rope. *They* were spacers.

Uma moved around so that her father could see the leak for himself through her helmet camera. The vapor trail was greenish-white in color.

"Why is the plume that color?" Uma asked. "We're not over the agriculture sector."

"No, but there are feed pipes underneath the hull that go to the biosuit factory. It looks like one of the supplementary chlorophyll lines has been pierced. This is going to need some major downtime and a full maintenance squad working inside and outside of the hull. Can you get a closer look?"

Uma edged closer to the leak. "Are you getting this?"

"Not much. The vapor is blocking my view. Can you see anything?"

"The hole is shaped like a shallow cone, with what looks like a pinhole at the end. It doesn't look serious —" She stopped speaking because she noticed some of the hull material crumbling away from the edges of the cone.

"Hey, Dad, would chlorophyll react with the hull material?"

"What do you mean?"

"Eat away at its structure, for example. It looks pretty crumbly here." Uma took some of the material between her right hand's thumb and forefinger and held it up for the camera.

"I see what you mean. I think I better tag this as urgent. And you'd better back away—"

But even as he spoke the leak suddenly became a small volcano. Uma didn't have time to cry out as a jet of green gas shot out, hitting her helmet. She jerked backward automatically, realizing too late that the hull material under her left hand was giving way. Arms flailing, her helmet's visor misted over with condensation, she banged into the hull with a bone-jarring crash. Then she tumbled away from the station.

"Uma! Uma! What's happening?"

Uma didn't know. Panic rose in her throat.

Calm down! she warned herself. She closed her eyes and concentrated on her breathing, making sure it was even and normal. As she regained control of her lungs, her heartbeat slowed. The biosuit, registering the change in Uma's pulse, reduced its production of oxygen.

Uma wiped the mist off her visor. She was spinning head over heels. The space station flashed into view and then disappeared with sickening speed. She closed her eyes again to stop feeling dizzy and reached for her belt. She used the small gas pack to send out a jet in the opposite direction of her spin.

Uma opened her eyes again. She was still turning, but more slowly now. She used quick blasts of the jet pack to stop the spin completely and orient herself toward the space station. Now she could see how far she was from the station and how quickly she was still moving away from it.

This is not good, she told herself.

"Uma!" her father cried. "Are you okay?"

"I'm adrift, Dad. The pinhole suddenly got bigger. I was caught by the gas emission. I don't know what my exact velocity is, but I'm moving away from the station pretty fast."

"Can you activate your beacon?" he asked urgently. "I'll get a cargo scooter to pick you up."

Uma used her chin to jab the emergency transmitter located in her helmet. "It's sending now. Are you receiving the signal?"

"Loud and clear. Help is on its way, honey."

Uma reached for the jet pack again to slow her movement away from *Plato* and hopefully start moving her back again. There was the smallest of reactions and then nothing. She twisted her head around and saw that half of the pack was damaged. It must have happened when she crashed into the hull. Her mouth went dry.

"Uh, Dad, are you still getting a picture?"

"Yes. What's your velocity, now?"

"I'm trying to estimate it, but I think it's too fast for any cargo scooter."

There was a moment's silence. If the cargo scooter couldn't reach her, Uma was in serious trouble. The biosuit would protect her as long as she stayed in sunlight. But if she was moving away from the station at a high enough velocity, she would eventually move out of L1's small, saddle-shaped gravity well and fall under the influence of Earth's. In that case, not even a passenger shuttle would be able to reach her in time.

"Are there any shuttles scheduled during the next few hours?" Uma asked nervously.

"Hold on, I'm checking." Uma heard her father speak over *Plato's* intercom. "Not for another six hours. Then there's a ten-seater from Tranquillity Base on the moon."

"Six hours may be too long," Uma said slowly.

"Don't give up, honey. We'll find a way to get you back. That's a promise."

"And Maintenance always keeps its promises."

"Uma, your signal's starting to fade."

"Dad? Do you still hear me?"

"Honey, I'm not receiving you. Just hang on. Everything's going to be okay."

And then her father's voice faded away. Uma put a gloved hand on top of her helmet. Her low gain antenna was snapped in half. It had probably been damaged in the same accident that had wrecked the jet pack.

Uma swallowed hard. If the antenna was out of action, it meant *Plato* wouldn't be receiving the beacon signal anymore, either. *They won't be able to find me,* she thought. *I'm as good as dead.*

No! She shook her head angrily. *I'm not giving up. There must be some way to slow my velocity.*

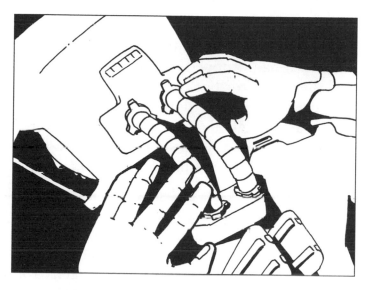

Then she thought, *the biosuit!* It produced oxygen as a waste product, oxygen she used to breathe. And oxygen was a gas! She reached behind her head to feel for the rebreather connector that attached to her helmet. She was about to twist it open when she remembered to get a visual bearing on both *Plato* and Earth. If she kept them in her sight in the same respective positions, she knew she would be heading in the right direction—back to the station.

Back home, she thought. She twisted the connector and pointed it in the direction opposite that of her movement away from *Plato*. She felt herself slow down, but then she lost sight of Earth. She redirected the nozzle slightly, and sighed with relief when the blue planet swung back into view.

Uma glanced at the oxygen level indicator inside the helmet. It had dropped alarmingly, and she twisted the connector back on, silently urging the oxygen level to rise. The biosuit was efficient, and soon she had enough air to repeat the maneuver. As she did so, her gloved hand slipped from the connector. She started to spin, and both *Plato* and Earth disappeared from view.

"No!" she shouted. She groped behind her helmet to find the hose. She found it and reconnected it, letting the oxygen reserve build up again. Spinning in space, Uma searched desperately for any sign of Earth or the station. Something flashed in the corner of her eye, then was gone. She waited a second, then saw it again. The silvery hull of *Plato*. She detached the hose, and with one thumb over the open nozzle, slowly killed her spin. Then she turned until *Plato* and Earth were back in sight in their original positions.

But had her accident pushed her closer or further

away from the station? She had no way of knowing. She swore softly under her breath.

And heard her father's voice. "Uma, is that you?"

"Dad!"

"The beacon signal is getting stronger, honey! I don't know how you did it, but you're actually coming toward the station. A cargo scooter's on its way."

Uma wanted to cry, but she stopped herself. Spacers didn't cry.

"Dad, this is the closest to Earth I ever want to get."

About the Illustrators

The Story Illustrator
Grant Gittus

Grant Gittus runs a small graphic design company. He has been interested in science fiction and fantasy since he was very young. He remembers dragging his mom to see *2001: A Space Odyssey*, and explaining it to her afterward. When Neil Armstrong landed on the moon, Grant remembers saying: "How come we're only on the *moon*? When do we go to the *stars*?"

The Cover Illustrator
Marc McBride

Marc McBride has illustrated covers for several magazines and children's books. Marc currently creates the realistic images for his covers using acrylic ink with an airbrush. To solve his messy studio problem, he plans to use computer graphics instead.